SO-AVG-894

U.S. ARMED FORCES

# U.S. AIR FORCE SPECIAL OPERATIONS

## JEREMY ROBERTS

LERNER PUBLICATIONS COMPANY / MINNEAPOLIS

## CHAPTER OPENER PHOTO CAPTIONS

Cover: Pilots hold their Pave Hawk helicopter in a hover to scan for Iraqi resistance fighters before dropping down to pick up two Air Force Special Operations airmen in 2004.

Ch. 1: A Pave Hawk helicopter raises two U.S. Air Force pararescue jumpers after the completion of an aid mission during Operation Iraqi Freedom in 2003.

Ch. 2: After talking with his parents and a guidance counselor, an air force candidate signs his enlistment papers in the presence of an air force recruiter *(right)*.

Ch. 3: A staff sergeant *(front center)* inspects a group of airmen during their basic training at Lackland Air Force Base in Texas. Following basic and additional training, some of these airmen will go on to be special operators.

Ch. 4: Special operators move a tent to a new location in Iraq in 2004. Special operators are stationed at bases around the world.

Copyright © 2005 by Jim DeFelice

All rights reserved. International copyright secured. No part of this book may be reproduced, stored in a retrieval system, or transmitted in any form or by any means— electronic, mechanical, photocopying, recording, or otherwise—without the prior written permission of Lerner Publications Company, except for the inclusion of brief quotations in an acknowledged review.

Lerner Publications Company
A division of Lerner Publishing Group
241 First Avenue North
Minneapolis, MN 55401 U.S.A.

Website address: www.lernerbooks.com

Library of Congress Cataloging-in-Publication Data

Roberts, Jeremy, 1956–
    U.S. Air Force Special Operations / by Jeremy Roberts.
      p.   cm. — (U.S. Armed Forces)
    Summary: Discusses the history of Air Force Special Operations units, as well as the organization's training program and what life is like in these specialized units.
    Includes bibliographical references and index.
    ISBN: 0–8225–1644–6 (lib. bdg. : alk. paper)
    1. United States. Air Force—Commando troops—Juvenile literature. 2. Special forces (Military science)—United States—Juvenile literature. [1. United States. Air Force— Commando troops. 2. Special forces (Military science)] I. Title. II. Series: U.S. Armed Forces (Series : Lerner Publications)
UG633.R625 2005
358.4—dc22                                2003020041

Manufactured in the United States of America
1 2 3 4 5 6 – JR – 10 09 08 07 06 05

# CONTENTS

**1** HISTORY ...................... 4

**2** RECRUITMENT .................. 22

**3** TRAINING ................... 32

**4** LIFE IN AIR FORCE
SPECIAL OPERATIONS ......... 42

structure chart ................. 55

timeline ...................... 56

glossary ...................... 58

famous people .................. 59

bibliography .................. 60

further reading ................. 60

websites ..................... 61

index ........................ 62

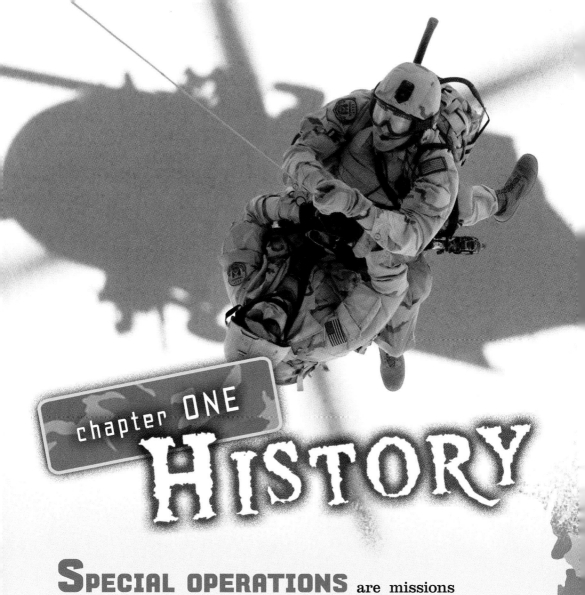

# chapter ONE
# HISTORY

**SPECIAL OPERATIONS** are missions that are out of the ordinary, or unlike conventional warfare. In conventional warfare, large groups of forces fight over a large area. In a conventional battle, armies try to push back the enemy and take over its land. Special operations often use smaller groups of highly trained soldiers. Special operations often take place in secret, inside enemy territory.

U.S. Air Force Special Operations units work in small groups. They have many jobs. Some use helicopters and airplanes to carry other special operations forces such as Army Rangers behind enemy lines. Others fly gunships (heavily armed aircraft) to attack the enemy at night. They fly special airplanes to jam radio signals. But Air Force Special Operations troops, or operators, also fight on the ground. Combat control technicians, or combat control team members (CCTs), help aircraft find enemy targets. Pararescue jumpers (PJs), or pararescuemen, are trained to survive, fight, and rescue people in the wilderness or inside enemy territory. All are members of the U.S. Air Force Special Operations Command (AFSOC).

Special operations missions are difficult and dangerous. U.S. Air Force special operators are the air force's elite—the best of the best. They are some of the toughest, best-trained soldiers and airmen in the world.

## THE FIRST SPECIAL OPERATION

In 1914 World War I (1914–1918) began in Europe. Great Britain, France, Italy, Russia, and many other countries fought against Germany, Austria-Hungary, and their allies.

A PJ helps secure a landing zone in Iraq in 2004. In addition to medical and rescue aid, PJs also are trained to fight.

5

In 1917 the United States entered the war on the side of Great Britain and its allies. The U.S. military did not have any Air Force Special Operations units. In fact, the United States did not even have a separate air force. U.S. warplanes were part of the U.S. Army. But in October 1918, U.S. pilots performed a mission similar to a modern-day special operation. A group of U.S. soldiers were cut off from their unit and lost in the woods of the Argonne Forest of France. Enemy soldiers were all around them. The U.S. troops had no food or supplies. Without help, they would surely die or be captured by the Germans.

The U.S. Army's 50th Aero Squadron sent out airplanes to look for the Americans. The aircraft carried supplies of food and other items. One of the planes finally spotted the troops. The pilot, Lieutenant Harold Goettler, flew low and slow to make sure he had the troops' location right. Meanwhile, the plane's observer, Lieutenant Erwin Bleckley, marked the spot on the map. Suddenly, German bullets hit the plane. Goettler managed to steer the plane back toward friendly territory before dying. The plane crashed. Bleckley soon died. But thanks to the efforts of the 50th Aero Squadron, the ground troops were rescued.

## WORLD WAR II

When Nazi Germany invaded Poland in 1939, the nations of Europe once again went to war. The conflict came to be known as World War II (1939–1945). At the start of the war, Great Britain, France, and the Soviet Union fought against Germany, Italy, and Japan. Japan

The USS *Arizona* burns and sinks after the Japanese attack on Pearl Harbor, Hawaii, on December 7, 1941. The attack drew the United States into World War II.

attacked and occupied China and other Asian countries. On December 7, 1941, Japanese aircraft attacked U.S. Navy and Army bases in the Hawaiian Islands. As a result, the United States joined the war against Japan, Germany, and Italy.

During World War II, British military leaders trained small groups of men for special operations inside enemy territory. The British called these troops commandos. Commando operations were usually covert, or secret. They scouted enemy territory or made attacks on difficult targets.

Commandos had to know how to sneak through an area without being noticed. They learned how to survive on their own for weeks or longer. Commandos also had to know how to use explosives to blow up a target such as a bridge or a building.

The U.S. military created its own special operations units to fight in Europe. Some were called Rangers. They trained and fought like British commandos. Other special operators were more like spies than soldiers. They worked for the Office of Special Services, or OSS.

Getting commandos into enemy territory was difficult. The U.S. Army Air Forces used B-24 Liberator

British commandos at a secret location in the United Kingdom during World War II. U.S. Rangers received some of their training from the more experienced British commandos during the war.

## THE B-24

The B-24 Liberator bomber was an important aircraft of World War II. Powered by four engines, the B-24 carried a crew of 10. It had machine guns for self-defense. B-24s could reach a maximum speed of about 300 miles an hour and carried 8,000 pounds of bombs.

bombers for the job. To make them hard to see at night, they painted the B-24s black. The planes usually flew at night and in stormy weather. The B-24s dropped commandos and supplies by parachute into enemy territory.

## AIR COMMANDOS

British and U.S. special operations forces also fought against the Japanese in the Asian countries of China and Burma (modern-day Myanmar) during the war. Among these special operators was the U.S. Army's 1st Air Commando Group. Air commandos used the C-47 Dakota, a cargo aircraft, to bring supplies to the soldiers on the ground. They also carried soldiers to the battlefield. The planes landed at rough airfields or dropped troops by parachute.

In August 1943, air commandos performed one of the first pararescue missions. An army cargo plane had mechanical problems, forcing its crew and passengers to bail out. They landed in the thick jungle near the border of China and Burma. Some of the men were hurt. But the thick jungle made it hard to deliver help by land.

Lieutenant Colonel Don Fleckinger and two soldiers volunteered to parachute down to treat the wounded. The three men used their first aid training to care for the injured until they could be rescued by land.

Air commandos also fought the enemy. They used B-25 Mitchell bombers to provide close air support to help ground troops during battle. The bombers used machine guns and cannons to fire at enemy ground soldiers. Besides C-47s and B-25s, air commandos flew fighters and small airplanes. They even used an early helicopter, the Sikorsky YR-4.

Germany and Japan surrendered in 1945. World War II was over. Special operations forces were still new. But it was clear that aircraft would continue to help them accomplish their mission.

## THE SIKORSKY YR-4

In March 1944, an experimental helicopter called the Sikorsky YR-4 carried out the first helicopter rescue ever. The air commando helicopter flew behind Japanese lines in Burma to rescue three British soldiers and a pilot who had been trapped there.

## AIR RESUPPLY AND COMMUNICATIONS

In 1947 the U.S. Army Air Forces became the United States Air Force (USAF). The air force was responsible for many special air missions, such as dropping troops and supplies behind enemy lines. During the Korean War (1950–1953), the air force adapted B-29 Superfortress bombers to perform these covert missions. A special hatch was added to the underside of the airplane. Soldiers jumped out of the hatch to parachute behind enemy lines. Small groups of soldiers were sent to spy on enemy forces or to help local people to fight the enemy. Commandos also attacked targets such as ammunition storehouses or communications networks.

## HELICOPTERS

Infiltration, or inserting troops in a combat area, was difficult. But picking them up from enemy territory, or exfiltration, was even harder. Airplanes such as the B-29 needed long runways to take off and land. They could not take off and land in the middle of enemy territory. During the Korean War, the air force and army started using helicopters for special operations. Helicopters can hover in place and land in a small area. They work well for both infiltration and exfiltration missions.

Meanwhile, the air force was already using helicopters for other missions. It created the 2157th Air Rescue Service to rescue airmen after their aircraft had been shot down. Rescuers from the 2157th parachuted from aircraft to get to downed airmen quickly and secretly.

An H-5 Dragonfly touches down during the Korean War in 1952. During the Korean War, pilots flew the H-5 for patient transport and rescue operations.

In January 1953, the U.S. Air Force began training teams to help guide aircraft during combat. The teams prepared rough airfields and placed special radios and lights to help aircraft take off and land safely. They also acted as ground controllers, helping pilots to avoid midair collisions. These ground controllers, sometimes called CCTs, soon became important special operators.

## VIETNAM

In the late 1960s and early 1970s, the United States fought alongside South Vietnam against North Vietnam. The U.S. Air Force formed the 4400th Tactical Combat Crew Training Squadron to perform special operations missions. Nicknamed Jungle Jim

The air force used a number of helicopters during the Vietnam War, including special versions of the UH-1 Huey *(above)*. Originally built for the U.S. Army, the Huey was very reliable.

RESCUING CIVILIANS

Air force pilots and crewmen don't just work in combat situations. PJs help save civilians (people who aren't in the military) who are hurt in airplane crashes or in other accidents in hard-to-reach areas. In the 1970s, PJs helped pick up astronauts who had "splashed down"—landed in the ocean after completing their space missions.

because it often worked in Vietnam's thick jungles, the 4400th handled many jobs.

Combat control teams helped direct air force bombing missions. Pararescuers dropped into enemy territory to rescue downed airmen and soldiers. One pararescue mission took place on March 18, 1969. Enemy forces shot down a U.S. Army helicopter in the Vietnamese jungle. An air force rescue helicopter dropped Sergeant Michael E. Fish into the area to rescue the injured crew. Under intense enemy fire, the PJ got four of the men into the rescue helicopter. But the pilot was trapped in the wreckage. So Fish stayed on the ground throughout the night to care for the pilot. Fish wasn't rescued for another 15 hours. Even with Fish's help, the pilot died.

As the war continued, new aircraft were used and some old ones were given new jobs. The air force placed a large machine gun in the fuselage, or body, of a C-47 cargo aircraft. The gun fired at the ground as the airplane circled above the enemy. The gun did a fearsome job. Soon more and bigger guns were added. A new close air support weapon—the gunship—was born. The air force labeled it the AC-47. These gunships performed many important missions during the Vietnam War.

In 1972 U.S. armed forces ended combat operations in Vietnam. Some U.S. forces stayed in the country to assist the South Vietnamese. The war between North and South Vietnam continued. In 1975 North Vietnamese troops swept into South Vietnam and took over the capital of Saigon to win the war. U.S. Air Force CCTs were some of the last to leave Saigon. They helped guide rescue missions taking Americans to safety.

## "PUFF" AND "SPOOKY"

AC-47 gunships often flew at night. Their powerful guns made them look like fire-breathing dragons. Soldiers called them "Puff" after a popular song, "Puff, the Magic Dragon." Other people called the gunships "Spooky"—and that's what they were to the enemy.

As North Vietnamese forces closed in on Saigon in 1975, U.S. forces and officials assisted citizens and diplomats in fleeing the city (above). Air force CCTs helped coordinate the massive airlift.

## TROUBLE IN IRAN

In 1979 a group of Iranians stormed the U.S. Embassy in Tehran, Iran. They captured about 70 Americans and held them hostage. The Iranian government refused to release the Americans. In the spring of 1980, U.S. president Jimmy Carter ordered the U.S. military to rescue the hostages. The rescue team included special operations teams from the air force, navy, and army.

A month before the raid, an Air Force Special Operations officer infiltrated Iran in a small airplane. He landed in the desert and scouted sites for a landing spot for the mission's aircraft.

When the mission began, some of the navy helicopters being used on the mission had mechanical problems. The commander decided to call off the operation. As the troops were leaving, one of the helicopters and a C-130 Hercules cargo plane collided. Eight soldiers were killed. No other rescue attempt was made, and the hostages were not released until the following year.

## NEW UNITS

The disaster in Iran helped convince U.S. military leaders to improve special operations units. The air force ordered newer versions of the C-130 Hercules, with improved weapons and tools. They also got their own long-range helicopters.

Military leaders also began reorganizing the armed services so they could work together in special operations. In March 1983, the air force placed all of its special operations forces under one command, under the control of a single officer.

This command was the 23rd Air Force, which included the 1st Special Operations Wing (SOW). The wing included gunships and helicopters. The wing also had airplanes that could bring troops and supplies behind enemy lines for covert operations. And it had aircraft that could be used for rescue operations. CCTs and PJs became members of special tactics squadrons. These squadrons, or small groups of men, could take on many different jobs. Often, members worked with other special operations forces, such as U.S. Army Rangers.

Months later, the 23rd Air Force went into action on the Caribbean island of Grenada. In the fall of 1983, Grenada's government was taken over by the country's military. U.S. officials feared that American students there would be taken hostage. AC-130 gunships and CCTs helped U.S. forces rescue the students. They also helped bring Grenada's elected leaders back to power.

Seven years later in Panama, U.S. forces invaded the country to capture Panamanian leader General Manuel Noriega.

## NOISE ANNOYS: OPERATION JUST CAUSE

During Operation Just Cause (1989–1990), Air Force Special Operations troops tried to get Panamanian leader Manuel Noriega to surrender without a fight. Crewmen attached speakers to an MH-53 Pave Low helicopter, then flew it over the house where Noriega was hiding. While the MH-53 hovered over the house, special operators blasted loud rock music. They hoped the awful noise might convince Noriega to give up. No one knows if the music made Noriega surrender. But it was one of the first times in air force history that rock music was officially used as a weapon. The military calls such missions psychological operations, or PSYOP.

The U.S. government accused Noriega of running an illegal drug smuggling operation. Many air force units took part in the operation.

In the late 1980s and early 1990s, the United States changed the way its military units were organized. Some of these changes helped special operators do their jobs better. The changes made it easier for special operators in different services, such as the army and air force, to work together. A new command called the U.S. Special Operations Command, or USSOCOM, took charge of all special operations units, whether they were part of the army, the navy, or the air force. In 1990 the air force established the Air Force Special Operations Command (AFSOC). AFSOC was part of USSOCOM, which included special operations units from every military branch.

## THE 1991 PERSIAN GULF WAR

In the early 1990s, AFSOC units were called into action in the Middle East. In 1990 Iraqi forces invaded Iraq's neighbor Kuwait. U.S. president George H. W. Bush ordered Iraqi forces to leave Kuwait. But Iraqi leader Saddam Hussein refused. Nations from all over the world formed a coalition, or group, to drive out the Iraqis.

The war began on January 17, 1991. The coalition attack plan was set to start with a massive night air raid against Iraqi targets. But the Iraqis had set up a radar station to track coalition aircraft. (Radar uses radio waves to detect aircraft.) U.S. forces had to destroy the radar station.

The U.S. Army's Apache attack helicopters had the firepower to destroy a radar station. But the Apaches did not have the special navigation equipment needed to find the target at night. The air force's MH-53 Pave Low helicopter did. But it didn't have the firepower

THE "HERKY BIRD"

Air Force Special Operations uses one basic airplane type, the C-130 Hercules. Each version of the Herky Bird is adapted for its special job. For example, AC-130Us are gunships, with special weapons in their cargo area. The MC-130E is designed to fly behind enemy lines at night and make it easy for troops to parachute from its back ramp.

to knock out a radar station. The helicopters worked together to do the job. The MH-53s led the Apache helicopter to the radar units. Then they peeled away as the Apaches moved up to blast them. The Persian Gulf War had begun.

A U.S. Air Force EC-130E, or Airborne Battlefield Command and Control Center (ABCCC). The ABCCC carries a 12-person special operations crew to provide direction and communications for air and land battles.

Other Air Force Special Operations units took part in the fighting. The 193rd Special Operations Wing flew a special PSYOP version of the C-130, known as EC-130 Commando Solo. Commando Solo broadcast radio programs calling on Iraqi soldiers to surrender. Other Air Force Special Operations forces dropped fliers to enemy troops to tell them how to surrender safely.

Another version of the C-130, known as the Airborne Battlefield Command and Control Center helped direct airplanes on bombing and close air support missions. AC-130 gunships also provided firepower during several battles. The coalition drove Saddam's forces out of Kuwait in just six weeks.

## FIGHTING TERRORISM

In 1993 U.S. special operators were sent to arrest a warlord in the East African nation of Somalia. The mission turned deadly when the warlord's fighters fired on the commandos and shot down an army helicopter. The helicopter's commandos and crew were trapped. Technical Sergeant Timothy A. Wilkinson, a pararescueman with the 24th Special Tactics Squadron, helped rescue them. Wounded himself, he managed to care for those who were hurt more seriously. For his bravery, he was awarded a medal, the Air Force Cross.

On September 11, 2001, terrorists struck the United States. They hijacked airliners and crashed them into the World Trade Center towers in New York City and into the U.S. military headquarters at the Pentagon near Washington, D.C. A fourth hijacked plane crashed in Pennsylvania. U.S. forces went to war to root out the al-Qaeda terrorists who had planned the attacks. U.S. troops invaded the Central Asian nation of Afghanistan, where the Taliban government allowed al-Qaeda to live and train. Special operations troops, including air force CCTs, parachuted into the hilly Afghan countryside. They directed bombing missions against al-Qaeda and Taliban targets. Within weeks the two groups were on the run and a new Afghan government was being set up.

In 2003 U.S. leaders again turned their attention to Saddam Hussein and Iraq. The Iraqi ruler had not honored his agreement to disarm his military after the 1991 Persian Gulf War. U.S. leaders said that Saddam was producing dangerous weapons that might threaten the United States and other countries. The United States joined with Great Britain to remove Saddam from power. They invaded Iraq and chased Saddam from Baghdad, the capital. Air Force Special Operations personnel and aircraft played an important role in the fight. CCTs helped guide attack planes to enemy targets. Aerial gunships pounded enemy positions. MC-130

LONG-DISTANCE FLYING

The world's record for the longest C-130 flight—and one of the longest-ever nonstop flights—is held by two special operations AC-130U gunships. In 1997 the planes flew for 36 hours from Hurlburt Field in Florida to Taegu Air Base in South Korea.

The term *special operations* has a lot of nicknames. An easy one to remember is SpecOp, which is just a shortening of special operations.

transports dropped special operators and supplies behind enemy lines. PJs stood by for rescue missions. Saddam's government was removed from power in three weeks.

After the downfall of the Iraqi government, air force special operators remained on the job. Gunships were used to fight back when guerrillas (groups of fighters that launch surprise attacks against

An antiterrorism special operator prepares to enter a building in Afghanistan to search for Taliban weapons in 2003.

an army or government) attacked U.S. troops. Air Force Special Operations planes flew army special operators around the country as they hunted for Saddam. Air Force Special Operations forces were part of the task force that captured Saddam in December 2003.

In Afghanistan air force special operators helped the new government fight rebels who wanted to overthrow it. The war against terrorists continued in 2004, as special operations troopers hunted for terrorists in the mountains between Afghanistan and Pakistan. As in Iraq, AC-130 gunships fired at enemy hideouts. CCTs helped direct attack planes on bombing missions. And special operations transports carried troops into dangerous areas.

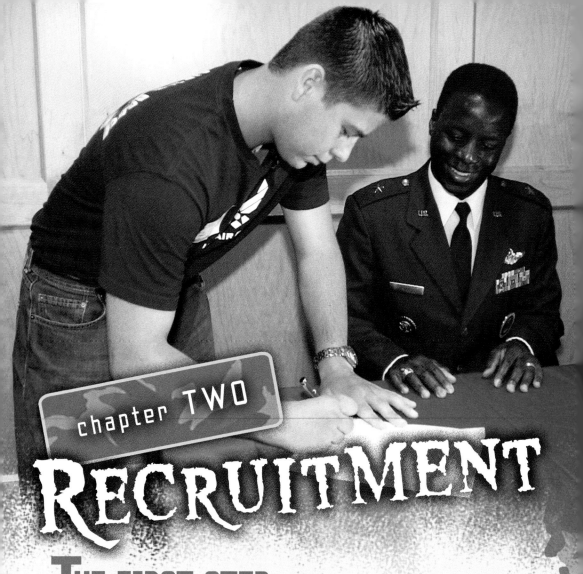

# chapter TWO

# RECRUITMENT

**THE FIRST STEP** to joining U.S. Air Force Special Operations is to enlist in, or join, the U.S. Air Force. After becoming an air force member, qualified persons can train for jobs in Air Force Special Operations. Some air force personnel train for special operations units as soon as they become air force members. Others may serve in other jobs in the air force before training for special operations.

Most enlistees who want to serve in special operations must be U.S. citizens. Enlistees must be

18 years old or older, although 17-year-olds can sign up with their parents' permission. People who are not yet U.S. citizens can also join the air force, as long as they plan to become a citizen and meet the other requirements.

Just like the other branches of the U.S. military, the air force has two different career paths—one for officers and one for enlisted personnel. As a general rule, officers are the commanders and leaders of units. But experienced enlisted men and women who earn the rank of sergeant also work in leadership roles. Both officers and enlisted men and women serve in U.S. Air Force Special Operations. But certain jobs—such as pilots, for example—are only open to officers. Others, such as PJs, are only open to enlisted personnel.

The U.S. Air Force is divided between active-duty wings, or units, and part-time branches. About 350,000 men and women serve in the active-duty air force.

Men and women of the air force security forces. The security forces offer one of the many career paths in the U.S. Air Force.

Another 250,000 serve part-time as reservists in Air Force Reserve and National Guard units. Most reservists hold civilian jobs or attend school. During peacetime, Air Force Reserve and National Guard units train and do missions only part-time. During an emergency, such as wartime, reservists can be called to full-time duty. The active duty, reserve, and National Guard parts of the air force have special operations units. But most Air Force Special Operations personnel are on active duty.

## ASVAB

The ASVAB is a multiple-choice test. The answers show the test-taker's skills and interests.

Here's a sample question:

A magnet will attract:

A. water

B. a flower

C. a cloth rag

D. a nail

(The answer is D, a nail.)

## AIRMEN: ENLISTED PERSONNEL

In the air force, enlisted personnel are called airmen. (Even women are called airmen.) Enlisted candidates must have a high school diploma. They also must take the Armed Services Vocational Aptitude Battery (ASVAB). This test covers math, science, mechanical, electronic, and language skills. U.S. Air Force counselors use the results to match air force jobs to a candidate's skills and interests. Candidates sign contracts agreeing to serve for at least four years as a full-time airman or for eight years as a part-time air force reservist.

Many of the jobs in U.S. Air Force Special Operations units are the same or very similar to other air force jobs. For example, aircraft maintenance is the

Women are not allowed in U.S. combat units yet, except as pilots or as crew members of warships. So women cannot serve as PJs or CCTs.

same throughout air force units. But other jobs, such as aerial gunner on an MH-53J Pave Low special operations helicopter, are only available in Air Force Special Operations units.

Most air force special operators need to learn their jobs at special air force schools or through other training. CCT and PJ are two of the elite Air Force Special Operations jobs. Enlisted men and women can try out for these jobs as long as they have a good score on the ASVAB, good eyesight and health, and the ability to pass very difficult physical fitness tests. The jobs are very demanding and take a long time to learn. The air force usually only allows men under the age of 28 to volunteer for these jobs.

This airman chose to train as an aerial gunner on special operations Pave Low helicopters.

# UNIFORMS

**LIKE THE OTHER** military branches, everyone in the U.S. Air Force wears a uniform while on duty. The air force has a long list of rules describing how men and women must dress while on duty. The booklet on air force rules and regulation is 145 pages—nearly three times as long as this book!

## SERVICE, OR "DRESS BLUE," UNIFORM

The dress blue uniform *(right)* is the formal air force uniform worn on important occasions. This uniform is a blue coat and pants, worn with a white or light blue button-down shirt and a tie.

## BLUES

Some air force personnel wear a semiformal uniform, called "blues" *(left),* for everyday jobs. Women can choose between skirts and trousers, unless they are marching, when they must wear trousers.

## BATTLE DRESS UNIFORM, OR BDU

Battle dress uniforms are everyday wear for military personnel. In the U.S. Air Force, BDUs have a camouflage pattern. This BDU *(left)* has a desert camouflage pattern. Its colors and patterns are designed to blend in with deserts, making a person harder to see.

## FLIGHT SUIT

Aircrews usually wear one-piece flight suits *(right).* They are made of a fabric that helps to protect them in case of a fire. In combat, especially on gunships, crews wear helmets and bulletproof flak vests for protection. Special radio headphones allow crew members to talk to each other, even in the loudest planes.

## OFFICERS

U.S. citizens who have a college degree or who are planning to attend college can become an officer candidate. The U.S. Air Force offers three different officer training programs: the Air Force Academy, the Reserve Officer Training Corps (ROTC), and the Officer Training School (OTS).

Before joining an officer training program, officer candidates must earn high scores on standardized tests such as the Scholastic Aptitude Test (SAT) or on the Air Force Officer Qualifying Test. They must also show that they have the ability to lead others and to learn new things quickly. Candidates must also be in excellent physical condition.

The Air Force Academy in Colorado Springs, Colorado, trains many of the air force's future officers. It is similar to the army's U.S. Military Academy at West Point, New York, and the U.S. Naval Academy at Annapolis, Maryland. The Air Force Academy is one of the top schools in the United States. Graduates

AT THE TOP

The top general of the air force is called the air force chief of staff. The chief of staff is a member of the Joint Chiefs of Staff (JCS), a group of the highest-ranking military leaders from each branch of the military. The JCS reports to the president of the United States on military matters.

The first female students entered the Air Force Academy in June 1976. Since then, many women have become important members of the air force's command structure.

An upper-class cadet (advanced student) barks out orders to new cadets at the U.S. Air Force Academy *(top)*. New rules at the academy, however, forbid unnecessary yelling at cadets. A Junior ROTC cadet *(below)* makes his way through a muddy obstacle course.

become air force officers and agree to serve full-time for four years.

ROTC programs are available at many high school and college campuses across the country. The program trains the air force's future officers and helps them pay for college. ROTC students (called cadets) take military courses as well as their civilian college courses. In return, the student agrees to serve in the air force after graduation. They can choose to serve full-time for 4 years or part-time for up to 10 years after graduation.

Enlisted personnel who already have a college degree can apply for a 12-week Officer Training School. Graduates of the challenging OTS become officers in the U.S. Air Force. Some move on to join Air Force Special Operations.

## OFFICERS IN SPECIAL OPERATIONS

Air force officers can apply for many types of jobs in special operations. Many serve as pilots. Officers of the 193rd Special Operations Wing plan psychological warfare operations. Their goal on a PSYOP mission might be to get the enemy to surrender without

A copilot checks her aircraft's flight systems before takeoff. Many Air Force Special Operations members are pilots.

AIR FORCE SONG:
Off we go into the wild blue yonder,
Climbing high into the sun;
Here they come zooming to meet our thunder,
At 'em boys, Give 'er the gun!
  (Give 'er the gun now!)
Down we dive, spouting our flame from under,
Off with one heck of a roar!
We live in fame or go down in flame. Hey!
Nothing'll stop the U.S. Air Force!

shooting or to reassure people in a disaster area that help is on the way. Weather officers work in every unit, providing forecasts for future operations. Officers also supervise AFSOC's special tactics squadrons.

Once people have enlisted in the air force, they must pass a difficult training program to become air force members. Once this basic training is completed, those who want to join Air Force Special Operations must go through additional and more demanding training. Only the best will make the cut.

# chapter THREE

# TRAINING

**O**NCE AN ENLISTED candidate is accepted
into the U.S. Air Force, he or she begins basic military
training. The air force holds basic training, or boot
camp, at Lackland Air Force Base near San Antonio,
Texas. The program lasts six and one-half weeks. Both
full-time personnel and reservists usually begin their
air force careers with boot camp.

Male recruits start out by getting a haircut. They have
their heads shaved. Women are allowed to have long hair
as long as it is neat and can be braided in less than two

minutes. The style of all recruits' hair gives them a similar look. Instead of separate individuals, each recruit is one member of a team. They are assigned to a class, or flight, of 30 to 60 people. Throughout basic training, recruits will learn to work as a team, doing most activities together.

Recruits learn to shoot weapons, follow a commander's orders, march in step, and many other skills. New recruits spend much of their time in physical fitness training. They exercise, climb ropes, and practice combat missions on obstacle courses. At the end of the program, recruits must pass a physical test to be accepted as airmen.

The final week of boot camp is called Warrior Week. All the recruits are housed in tents in a special camp. The instructors act as the enemy and attack the camp. To defend the camp, the recruits must put their training and teamwork skills to the test.

Recruits who make it through basic training participate in a graduation ceremony. Wearing their blue and white U.S. Air Force uniforms, they march on parade in front of superior officers, friends, and family.

Instructors test recruits' skills and push them to their limits during Warrior Week *(above)*.

After graduation, they are officially airmen. Graduates who want to join the U.S. Air Force Special Operations move on to train for their jobs.

## SPECIAL TACTICS

The most specialized and dangerous jobs in Air Force Special Operations belong to the special tactics squadrons. These jobs include CCTs and PJs. Candidates for special tactics must be in excellent physical condition. To be accepted for training they must pass some tough physical tests. The indoctrination (first) course for special tactics lasts for 12 weeks. It begins with weight training and exhausting runs. This exercise soon seems easy. By week three, candidates are crawling through a muddy

An air force instructor shows a group of PJ candidates how to adjust parachute rigging before a test jump.

PJS

Pararescuers are called PJs because of the initials entered in the flight logs that record the crew on a mission or flight. A very simple system is used, with the fewest initials possible to stand for a person's job. Pilots are entered in the logs as Ps, for example. The pararescuemen's full title is "pararescue jumper," which shows that he knows how to parachute from an aircraft. This is shortened to PJ.

training course. The course is so tough that many people drop out in the early weeks.

The indoctrination course is followed by more classes held at different military bases. Parachute training takes place at Fort Bragg, North Carolina. Here candidates learn how to jump out of aircraft. The training includes advanced instruction in controlling parachutes, night jumps, and high-altitude operations. Candidates also take air traffic control training at Keesler Air Force Base in Mississippi and underwater combat diving at Key West Naval Air Station in Florida.

Instruction continues as the CCTs and PJs learn their craft. Special schools such as the Combat Control School at Pope Air Force Base in North Carolina and Combat Survival School at Fairchild Air Force Base in Washington teach controllers valuable skills. They learn how to turn a flat piece of land into a workable airstrip for landing aircraft. PJs spend 24 weeks learning how to care for the wounded in combat conditions. When they are finished, PJs can treat anything from a broken arm to a heart attack. They will learn how to use different medicines and are even trained to perform surgery, if necessary.

# TOOLS OF THE TRADE

**U.S. AIR FORCE SPECIAL OPERATIONS** use a variety of equipment, from airplanes to helicopters, to heavy machine guns to small firearms. Many of its aircraft are adapted for special operations missions.

## PAVE LOWS

The MH-53J Pave Low III *(left)* is designed for search-and-rescue and infiltration missions. The Pave Low crew can see in the dark, thanks to a special kind of radar. Gunners provide cover with large machine guns and slightly smaller miniguns.

## PAVE HAWKS

The Sikorsky H-60 Black Hawk is a workhorse for the U.S. military. There are many, many models. The HH-60 Pave Hawk *(right)* is a special operations version of the Black Hawk. The machine gun-armed Pave Hawk holds a lot of fuel for long-distance missions.

## HERKY BIRDS

There are many versions of the C-130 Hercules, including AC-130 gunships. The latest version is the AC-130U, nicknamed Spooky *(left).* It uses a 25mm Gatling gun (a high-speed, rotating multiple-barrel cannon), a single-barrel, rapid-fire 40mm cannon, and a 105mm howitzer. All of the weapons are guided by sensors in the plane.

The MC-130 versions of the Hercules drop special operations forces and supplies deep behind enemy lines. These Combat Talons have special navigation gear to help pilots fly them in the dark.

EC-130E Commando Solo aircraft are specially equipped to locate and jam enemy radio transmitters. At the same time, the crew aboard these planes can transmit radio and television messages to civilians and troops. The messages may urge people on the ground to surrender or cooperate with U.S. forces.

## M16 AND M4

The M4 *(right)* is an assault rifle—a high-powered, rapid-fire weapon. The M4 is a shorter, lighter version of the M16 assault rifle. Its length and weight make it easy to carry into combat, especially when jumping out of a plane or helicopter.

To become Air Force Special Operations members, candidates must graduate from all of the required military training courses. They are then invited to return to Lackland Air Force Base for a 12-week Combat Control/Pararescue Selection program, where candidates practice different kinds of combat situations to test their skills. The best of those soldiers then join a special tactics group. The training is so tough that fewer than one-third of all the candidates

## DROWNPROOF AIRMEN

Pararescuemen often have to make rescues at sea. Very early in their training, they must prove that they are "drownproof." PJs must show that they can swim for hours—even while carrying heavy gear. They also have to pass tests during which instructors harass them, even trying to take their swimming equipment. The idea is to make sure they won't panic in an emergency.

Pararescuemen practice an open-field rescue of a downed pilot as part of their ongoing training.

who start training for special operations actually earn the privilege to serve in a special operations unit.

## FIGHTING WEATHERMEN

Knowing the weather is an important part of combat planning. For example, bad weather might make it difficult for close air support aircraft to protect troops in battle. Poor conditions might also make parachute drops too dangerous. On the other hand, bad weather might provide cover for a unit planning a surprise attack.

To keep informed of weather conditions, the U.S. Air Force Special Operations Command has a Special Tactics Combat Weather Team. These airmen and officers must have already earned a civilian degree in meteorology (the science of studying and interpreting weather patterns) before entering the U.S. Air Force or while serving in the reserves. Combat weathermen are both meteorologists (people who study and predict weather) and special operations soldiers. They receive the same parachute, combat, and survival training as other special operations soldiers. Women are allowed in these units. But women are not allowed into combat or to go behind enemy lines.

## OFFICER TRAINING

Many special operations officers are pilots. They must volunteer for special operations. Commanders select them only after carefully checking their skills and past achievements. They come to special operations already knowing how to fly. However, they learn and practice new skills used in special operations. For example, a new pilot might know how to fly the C-130 Hercules.

A special operations Pave Low crew practice flying at night and launching flares (burning devices that produce bright light).

After joining special operations, the pilot learns how to fly at night at very low altitudes using special equipment. Pilots practice these skills again and again until they become second nature.

Not every officer in the air force is a pilot. Officers lead special tactics squadrons. In some cases, they train side by side with enlisted personnel and even take the same tests. Officers also receive special training to learn how to plan and lead rescue and combat-control missions. Other officers supervise enlisted men and women in jobs such as maintenance and supply. They help plan missions and make sure they succeed.

## U.S. AIR FORCE SPECIAL OPERATIONS SCHOOL

AFSOC personnel receive important training at the U.S. Air Force Special Operations School. Located at AFSOC headquarters at Hurlburt Field, Florida, the school has courses on many subjects. Both training and active-duty special operators from all of the U.S.

## LIFE AFTER SERVICE

Many young people join the air force to gain skills that they can use at other jobs later on. Many airlines, for example, hire former air force pilots. Airplane mechanics or "maintainers" are also in demand.

Training for special operations positions can also help prepare a person for a career after the military. Pararescue jumpers, for example, have special medical skills that are needed in hospitals and in paramedic rescue squads.

armed forces study at the school.

Students at the school learn the newest special operation tactics. Students also train in regional and cultural awareness. They study the historical, political, economic, and cultural situation in the world's different regions. This knowledge is very important to special operations troopers because they often work with people on missions in foreign lands.

Joining a unit is a major accomplishment. But the training doesn't end there. In many ways, it's just the beginning. To keep their skills sharp, units practice them regularly. They also learn new techniques and train on new equipment.

As part of the Air Force Special Operations Command, air force special operators often work and train with special operations units from other branches of the military. These missions are called joint operations. For example, CCTs may train or perform missions alongside U.S. Army Ranger troopers or U.S. Navy SEAL units.

# chapter FOUR
# LIFE IN AIR FORCE SPECIAL OPERATIONS

**ACTIVE-DUTY AIR FORCE** officers and airmen live on and near air bases in the United States and around the world. Many air bases are like small towns, with their own stores, post offices, and gyms. Some personnel live on base with their families, in special apartments and houses supplied by the military. Others live in homes nearby and go to work every day just like civilians.

Air force reservists work full-time at civilian jobs but spend a few hours a month training and working in the

## ARMY AIR FORCE

When the air force split from the army in 1947, it took all of its airplanes with it. The army flies only a few very small planes, mostly for transportation missions.

The army does have a special operations aviation unit, the 160th Special Operations Aviation Regiment (SOAR). This special group flies combat helicopters, including MH-47 Chinooks, MH-6 and AH-6 Little Birds, and MH-60 Black Hawks.

military. They also promise to serve full-time if the country is at war. The U.S. Air Force Special Operations has one reserve unit. Known as the 919th Special Operations Wing (919th SOW), it is located at Duke Field in Florida. The unit has more than 1,300 reservists from all over the country. Each year they come to the base for a two-week training camp and spend one weekend a month at the base. A small group of reservists work on the base full-time.

Descending from an air traffic control tower, this Air Force Special Operations reservist is practicing his rappelling skills while on active duty in Baghdad, Iraq.

About 12,500 men and women make up the U.S. Air Force Special Operations Command. AFSOC includes active-duty, Air Force Reserve, and National Guard units. Most AFSOC personnel are based at Hurlburt Field. AFSOC also has special operations units stationed overseas in Great Britain, Japan, and South Korea.

Wherever they are based, special operations personnel are always ready to go anywhere in the world on short notice. Special forces units are often the first ones called for combat or humanitarian aid missions. These units may spend weeks or even months at a time away from home.

AFSOC has about 160 aircraft. Most special operations aircraft are versions designed just for special operations missions. They include helicopters such as the MH-53 Pave Low and many specialized versions of the C-130 Hercules. About one-fifth of AFSOC's aircraft are stationed outside the United States.

An active-duty CCT practices blending into the background to avoid being seen.

Watchful for enemy forces, two CCTs call in key coordinates to their commanders for a close air strike.

## SPECIAL TACTICS

Only a few hundred men work for the air force's special tactics squadrons, but their jobs are extremely important. Special tactics teams include CCTs, pararescuers, and combat weathermen.

CCTs set up air assault landing zones, or landing areas for airplanes and helicopters. They use everything from explosives (for clearing out trees and other objects) to sophisticated electronic equipment to do the job. CCTs are also the air force's "eyes on the ground." They work on the ground to direct close air support. CCTs use equipment such as laser beams to mark enemy targets. Then they call in aircraft to destroy the targets. Combat controllers must be able to parachute from high altitudes carrying weapons and about 100 pounds of gear. CCT gear includes radios, night-vision goggles, and lights for guiding aircraft. The CCT motto is First There.

# INSIGNIA

**THE U.S. AIR FORCE** is organized by rank. A person of lower rank is required to follow the orders of someone of higher rank. For example, an airman, the lowest rank, is expected to follow the orders of a sergeant. A sergeant follows a captain's orders. A captain is required to follow the orders of a major or a colonel and so on. All air force personnel wear insignia to show their rank.

Most AFSOC personnel are either officers or higher-ranking enlistees, such as sergeants. Most air force pilots are officers. Enlisted special operations troopers earn higher ranks through their training and service experience.

## ENLISTED PERSONNEL

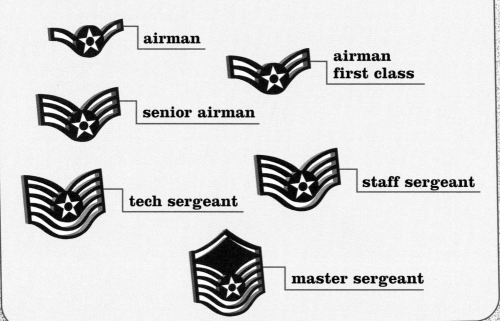

airman

airman first class

senior airman

tech sergeant

staff sergeant

master sergeant

# OFFICERS

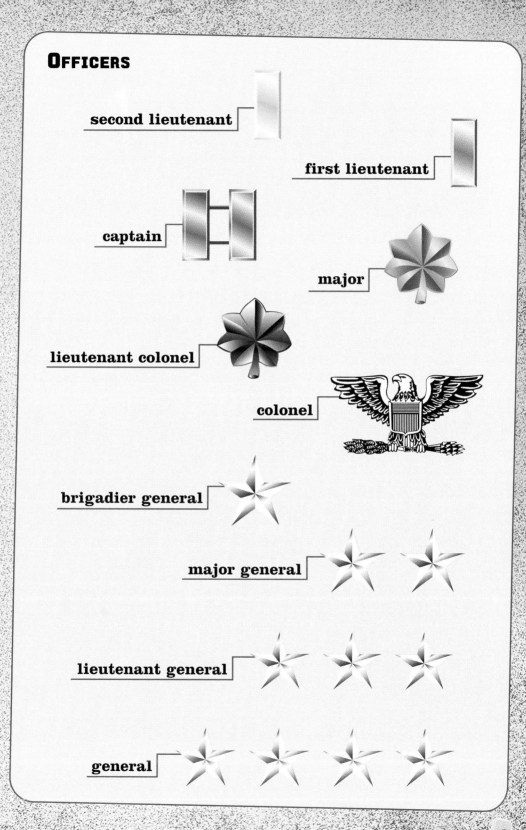

second lieutenant

first lieutenant

captain

major

lieutenant colonel

colonel

brigadier general

major general

lieutenant general

general

Pararescuers don't just rescue military people. PJs sometimes rescue civilians who have gotten lost in the wilderness or people at sea in sinking ships. Like CCTs, pararescuers must be able to parachute from high altitudes carrying lots of equipment. They even carry equipment that can be used to cut air crash victims out of aircraft wreckage. PJs have a tough and dangerous job. They must be able to work well in high-pressure situations. The PJ motto is That Others May Live.

Combat weathermen play an important role in planning missions. They often work inside enemy territory. They pass on weather information to military leaders. The leaders use the weather predictions to plan missions.

Two combat weathermen report weather conditions and wind speeds before an air assault *(top)*. PJs make a high-altitude jump from the back of an HC-130 Hercules aircraft *(bottom)*.

Combat weathermen also train other Air Force Special Operations Command members in collecting weather information. They are often dropped into hostile areas, so combat weathermen must be able to fight when necessary. AFSOC's 10th Combat Weather Squadron motto is Coela Bellatores, which means "weather warriors."

## OTHER MISSIONS

Air Force Special Operations has many other units, each with its own tasks. One of the most important is transporting, or inserting, special operations soldiers into enemy territory. The MC-130 Combat Talon aircraft are specially designed to fly behind enemy lines, where troops can secretly parachute to the ground. Two specially trained pilots fly the Combat Talon. An enlisted flight engineer looks after the airplane's mechanical system. Crewmen called loadmasters handle cargo in the rear of the aircraft.

Dropping men and heavy boxes of gear by parachute requires a great deal of planning and training. Crews learn how to drop gear in high winds and from high and low altitudes. Some Combat Talons even have a special hook that allows them to snag men who are on the ground and lift them into the airplane.

The air force also uses helicopters for insertion missions. The MH-53 Pave Low and the MH-60 Black Hawk have equipment that helps the crews see in the dark and move behind enemy lines. They are also equipped with extra-large fuel tanks (for long-range missions) and machine guns.

Air Force Special Operations jobs also include directing other aircraft. A special version of the C-130 known as the EC-130 ABCCC works as a flying headquarters. Controllers aboard the Airborne Battlefield Command and Control Center take radio information from ground units. They then direct airplanes on bombing and close air support missions. Another version of the C-130, EC-130 Commando Solo, flies on PSYOP missions. This plane's high-tech electronic equipment can broadcast on many radio and television channels. In 1991 it broadcast directions to Iraqi soldiers on how to surrender during the Persian Gulf War. Yet another type of C-130, EC-130 Compass Call aircraft, can interrupt, or jam, the enemy's radio and TV signals. Its crew can also detect where and when the enemy tries to jam its signals. This helps the crew find out where the enemy is.

Special operations crews sometimes perform humanitarian missions. Airmen have brought food, medicine, and other supplies to starving people in Africa, Bosnia, and northern Iraq. These jobs involve many of the skills and abilities needed on regular special operations missions.

## GUNSHIPS AND TESTING NEW EQUIPMENT

Close air support is also an important special operations' job. AC-130 Spooky gunships carry fourteen crew members. In addition to the pilot and copilot, five enlisted men handle the weapons. A fire control officer is in charge of the targeting equipment. AC-130s also have a flight engineer aboard to help the

A test flight of the Osprey. The tilting rotors (propeller engines) of the plane allow it to take off, land, and hover like a helicopter. The plane also has long-range flight capabilities.

pilots in case the equipment breaks down. These newer aircraft are armed with radar-aimed guns that can lock on to enemy targets even in the dark.

The 18th Flight Test Squadron is part of AFSOC. The squadron tests new equipment to see if it might be useful in special operations. Members of the squadron also test tactics, such as rescues.

The squadron also tests new aircraft. For example, the squadron has been testing different kinds of the V-22 Osprey. This aircraft has wings that tilt to face upward or forward. It can fly like an airplane and land like a helicopter. The Osprey is much faster and can fly much farther than helicopters. The Osprey will be a very important tool for special operations work.

Air Force Special Operations has many support people, including aircraft mechanics. Life Support Shop personnel keep flight suits and other gear ready to use. The aircrews and special tactics squadrons depend on a wide range of experts to accomplish their missions.

## THE FUTURE OF AIR FORCE SPECIAL OPERATIONS

The threat of terrorism in the United States and around the world has made special operations forces highly important. The U.S. military knows it must be prepared to move into trouble spots quickly. U.S. Air Force Special Operations forces are trained for these kinds of missions. They deliver troops and equipment to insertion points quickly and secretly. Once these troops are on the ground, they often need close air support from gunships. CCTs are needed to help other aircraft find enemy targets.

Natural disasters such as earthquakes kill hundreds of people every year. Floods and

An Air Force Special Operations unit quickly drops from a Pave Hawk into a combat zone in Iraq.

## BIG BOMBS

The air force has two very large bombs that it uses for special tasks. The BLU-82 Daisy Cutter and the 21,000-pound Massive Ordnance Air Blast (MOAB) are so huge they can only be dropped from the rear of an MC-130 cargo plane.

The Daisy Cutter can clear a large area in just a few seconds. It was first used in Vietnam to help clear the jungle for helicopter landings. Daisy Cutters have been used to destroy minefields—areas with explosive devices planted underground—large enemy bases, and bunkers (fortified underground bases). The newer, more powerful MOAB has been developed for the same purpose.

famine (severe food shortages) can threaten the lives of thousands. AFSOC personnel are trained to help in these emergencies.

## NEW EQUIPMENT

In the 2000s, one of the newest air force aircraft is unmanned. The Global Hawk is a long-range unmanned aerial vehicle (UAV), or remote control aircraft. It works as a reconnaissance plane, scouting behind enemy lines. While a team on the ground controls the Global Hawk, the aircraft sends video images of enemy operations. UAVs allow military leaders to scout the enemy without risking a pilot's life.

Future special operations soldiers may have their own personal UAVs that can supply information on what's going on around them. The U.S. military is testing "smart helmets" that have built-in computers and special video screens. They will give tomorrow's special operations soldiers instant information about the battlefield. Pararescuemen may carry miniature personal computers crammed with medical information in their kits.

AIR FORCE SPECIAL OPERATIONS COMMAND

This is the shield emblem of U.S. Air Force Special Operations Command. AFSOC's motto is Quiet Professionals, because its members are highly trained and often work in secret.

Meanwhile, researchers are working on new weapons for special operations soldiers. They are building high-energy weapons that may replace the AC-130U. These high-energy weapons use energy beams or even sound waves to blow up tanks and buildings. Instead of contacting gunships, combat controllers may call in laser strikes from jets above the battlefield or even from satellites. Whatever the future holds, special operations units will be there, on the cutting edge.

# STRUCTURE

**THE PRESIDENT OF THE** United States is commander in chief of all the U.S. armed forces. The secretary of defense is in charge of the armed forces and reports directly to the president. The Air Force Special Operations Command is led by a three-star general (lieutenant general). The command is divided into different squadrons, wings, and groups. Examples include the 16th Special Operations Wing based in Florida; the 352nd Special Operations Group, which handles special missions in Europe, Africa, and the Middle East; and the 353rd Special Operations Group in Asia. These and many other wings, squadrons, and groups—including the 720th Special Tactics Group, which is the air force's "first to serve" in combat locations around the world—make up the Air Force Special Operations Command.

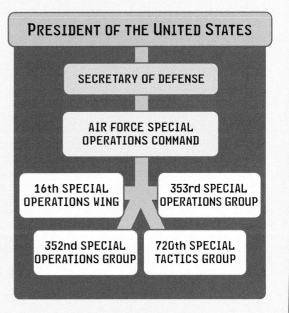

PRESIDENT OF THE UNITED STATES

SECRETARY OF DEFENSE

AIR FORCE SPECIAL OPERATIONS COMMAND

16th SPECIAL OPERATIONS WING

353rd SPECIAL OPERATIONS GROUP

352nd SPECIAL OPERATIONS GROUP

720th SPECIAL TACTICS GROUP

# TIMELINE

**1918** During World War I, commanders of the U.S. Army's 50th Aero Squadron send out airplanes on an airborne search-and-rescue mission, the first of its kind in U.S. military history.

**1941** The United States enters World War II, with the U.S. Army Air Forces playing a major role.

**1943** U.S. air units operating in Burma become the first airmen to be called air commandos.

**1947** The U.S. Air Force is formed as a separate branch of the military.

**1953** The U.S. Air Force trains the first combat air controllers to guide air drops.

**1961** An Air Force Tactical Air Command unit known as Jungle Jim starts up at Hurlburt Field, Florida. This is the start of modern U.S. Air Force Special Operations.

**1965** Air force units begin to play a large role in the Vietnam War. AC-47 "Puff the Magic Dragon" flying gunships are flown in combat for the first time.

**1967** AC-130 "Spectre" gunships begin to replace AC-47s.

**1980** An attempt to rescue American hostages in Iran ends in disaster. The lessons learned from this operation will help improve special operations forces.

**1983** The 23rd Air Force is formed. U.S. forces invade Grenada, receiving support from U.S. Air Force AC-130 gunships and other special operations units. Aerospace Rescue and Recovery units join special operations forces.

**1987** In an important reorganization of military structure, the U.S. Special Operations Command (USSOCOM) is formed.

**1989** U.S. forces invade Panama to remove the country's leader, Manuel Noriega. Air Force Special Operations' AC-130 gunships supply firepower, MC-130s refuel helicopters, and MH-53 helicopters play loud music to harass Noriega and other Panamanian leaders as part of a PSYOP mission.

**1990** The 23rd Air Force becomes Air Force Special Operations Command (AFSOC).

**1991** Coalition forces, led by the United States, drive Iraqi forces out of Kuwait. As the war begins, air force MH-53 Pave Lows act as pathfinders for other helicopters, showing them the way to their targets.

**2001** After the September 11 terrorist attacks in the United States, AFSOC units help to destroy al-Qaeda terrorist bases and the Taliban government in Afghanistan.

**2003** Air Force Special Operations participate in the invasion of Iraq to remove Saddam Hussein from power

**2004** Air Force Special Operations assist in the ongoing hunt for al-Qaeda and Taliban terrorists in Afghanistan.

# GLOSSARY

**combat control technician (CCT):** an Air Force Special Operations soldier trained to help guide airplanes in flight and while landing and taking off. Also called a combat controller.

**covert:** secret. Special operations missions are often called covert operations.

**enlisted:** a soldier from the airman to sergeant ranks. Most air force personnel are enlisted personnel.

**exfiltrate:** a military term for secretly removing troops behind enemy lines

**infiltrate:** a military term for secretly bringing, or inserting, soldiers into enemy territory. The air force uses many types of aircraft to insert special operations troops into enemy territory.

**insignia:** a badge or symbol to show military rank

**officer:** a person serving in the lieutenant to general ranks

**pararescue jumper (PJ):** an Air Force Special Operations soldier trained to help rescue people, often by parachuting into an area

**reconnaissance:** a military term for scouting, or looking at what the enemy is doing

# FAMOUS PEOPLE

**Colonel Charles A. Beckwith** (1929–1994) Born in Georgia, Colonel Beckwith served as a U.S. Army Special Forces officer and organized the U.S. Army's covert operations team Delta Force in the 1970s. He was in charge of the disastrous Operation Eagle Claw, the mission to rescue U.S. civilians being held hostage in Iran in 1980. After the disaster, recommendations by Beckwith and others helped Air Force Special Operations units get better equipment and a bigger role in special missions.

**Lieutenant Colonel Philip G. Cochran** (1910–1979) Born in Pennsylvania, Cochran served as a fighter pilot during World War II and helped organize and command the 1st Air Commando Group. He received medals from the British as well as the U.S. government for his service.

**Lieutenant Harold Goettler** (1890–1918) Born in Illinois, Lieutenant Goettler served as a U.S. Army pilot during World War I. Flying with Lieutenant Erwin Bleckley (1895–1918) as observer, he helped find lost U.S. soldiers, bringing them badly needed supplies. Both men died in the operation. Both Goettler and Bleckley were later awarded the Congressional Medal of Honor.

**Sergeant John L. Levitow** (1945–2000) Born in Connecticut, Levitow served aboard an AC-47 gunship in Vietnam. On February 24, 1969, Levitow's aircraft was hit by enemy fire. The explosion caused a member of the crew to drop a flare to light up the AC-47's target area. To keep the flare from setting off the plane's ammunition, Levitow jumped on the burning flare and smothered it with his body. He then threw it out of the airplane, saving his fellow crew members from certain death.

**Airman First Class William H. Pitsenbarger** (1945–1966) Born in Ohio, Airman Pitsenbarger served as a pararescueman during Vietnam. He lost his life carrying out the PJ motto, That Others May Live. On an operation near Cam My in Vietnam, he helped recover nine wounded men during a single day on April 11, 1966. Under heavy fire, he tried to get more men to safety while a helicopter returned with the wounded. He was killed when the enemy attacked. Pitsenbarger was later awarded the Congressional Medal of Honor for his heroic actions.

# BIBLIOGRAPHY

Alexander, David. *Tomorrow's Soldier.* New York: Avon Books, 1999.

Carney, John T., Jr., and Benjamin F. Schemmer. *No Room for Error.* New York: Ballantine Books, 2002.

Chinnery, Philip D. *Air Commando.* New York: St. Martin's Press, 1997.

Clancy, Tom, Carl Stiner, and Tony Koltz. *Shadow Warriors.* New York: G. P. Putnam's Sons, 2002.

Keaney, Thomas A., and Eliot A. Cohen. *Revolution in Warfare?* Annapolis, MD: Naval Institute Press, 1995.

Kelly, Orr. *From a Dark Sky: The Story of U.S. Air Force Operations.* New York: Simon and Schuster, 1996.

Morrow, John H., Jr. *The Great War in the Air: Military Aviation from 1909 to 1921.* Washington, DC: Smithsonian Press, 1993.

Perret, Geoffrey. *Winged Victory: The Army Air Forces in World War II.* New York: Random House, 1993.

Southworth, Samuel A., and Stephen Tanner. *U.S. Special Forces.* Cambridge, MA: DaCapo Press, 2002.

Walker, Greg. *At the Hurricane's Eye.* New York: Ivy Books, 1994.

Waller, Douglas C. *The Commandos.* New York: Simon and Schuster, 1994.

# FURTHER READING

Donovan, Sandy. *The U.S. Air Force.* Minneapolis: Lerner Publications Company, 2005.

Feldman, Ruth Tenzer. *The Korean War.* Minneapolis: Lerner Publications Company, 2004.

———. *World War I.* Minneapolis: Lerner Publications Company, 2004.

Goldstein, Margaret J. *World War II—Europe.* Minneapolis: Lerner Publications Company, 2004.

Green, Michael. *Night Attack Gunships.* Bloomington, MN: Capstone Press, 2003.

Holden, Henry M. *Air Force Aircraft.* Berkeley Heights, NJ: Enslow Publishers, 2001.

Kennedy, Robert C. *Life as an Air Force Fighter Pilot.* New York: Children's Press, 2000.

Levy, Debbie. *The Vietnam War.* Minneapolis: Lerner Publications Company, 2004.

Williams, Barbara. *World War II—Pacific.* Minneapolis: Lerner Publications Company, 2005.

## WEBSITES

*Air Force Link*
   <http://www.af.mil>
   The official site of the U.S. Air Force has a variety of basic information, including how to join the air force. The site also features links to other air force sites.

*Air Force Link: Fact Sheets*
   <http://www.af.mil/factsheets>
   Read the fact sheets to learn more about AFSOC, CCTs, combat weathermen, PJs, and the many specialized aircraft used by AFSOC.

*ASVAB Career Exploration Program*
   <http://www.asvabprogram.com>
   Learn more about the Armed Services Vocational Aptitude Battery program, which many people—both military and civilian—use to find careers that match their skills and interests.

*U.S. Air Force: Cross into the Blue*
   <http://www.airforce.com>
   Find out more about air force careers, training, how to join, and life in the air force at this official U.S. Air Force site.

*U.S. Air Force Museum*
   <http://www.wpafb.af.mil/museum/index.htm>
   This is the official website of the U.S. Air Force Museum at Wright-Patterson Air Force Base in Dayton, Ohio. The site has pictures of many historical aircraft, as well as historical information.

# INDEX

Afghanistan, 20, 21, 57
aircraft, 10, 11, 16, 20, 35; AC-47
    gunships, 5, 13, 14, 16, 56, 57;
    AC-130 gunships, 16, 19, 21, 37,
    50, 56; AC-130U, 18, 20, 37, 54;
    EC-130 Commando Solo, 37, 50;
    EC-130 Compass Call, 50; EC-
    130E (ABCCC), 18, 19, 50; Global
    Hawk, 53; MC-130 Combat Talon,
    49; MC-130E, 18, 21, 37, 53; V-22
    Osprey, 51. *See also* helicopters
Air Force Academy, 28, 29
Air Force Officer Qualifying Test,
    28
Air Force Reserve, 24, 44
airmen, 24, 25, 33, 34, 39, 42, 46,
    50
Armed Services Vocational Aptitude
    Battery (ASVAB), 24, 25

bases, 42; Duke Field, 43; Fairchild
    Air Force Base, 35; Fort Bragg,
    35; Hurlburt Field, 44, 56;
    Keesler Air Force Base, 35; Key
    West Naval Air Station, 35;
    Lackland Air Force Base, 32,
    38; Pope Air Force Base, 35
Beckwith, Charles A., 59
Bush, George H. W., 17

Carter, Jimmy, 15
Combat Control/Pararescue
    Selection program, 38
Combat Control School, 35
combat control technicians (CCTs),
    12, 14, 16, 25, 34; missions, 4,
    5, 20, 21, 41, 45, 52; motto, 45;
    training, 35, 41, 44. *See also*
    special tactics squadrons
Combat Survival School, 35
combat weathermen, 39, 45, 48–49;
    10th Combat Weather
    Squadron, 49
commandos, 7–9, 19; air
    commandos, 9–10, 56, 59

Goettler, Harold, 6, 59
Grenada, 16, 56

helicopters, 11, 13, 15, 16; Apache,
    18; HH-60 Pave Hawk, 4, 36,
    52; MH-47 Chinook, 43; MH-53
    Pave Low, 16, 18, 25, 36, 40,
    44, 49, 56, 57; MH-6/AH-6 Little
    Bird, 43; MH-60 Blackhawk,
    36, 43, 49. *See also* aircraft
Hussein, Saddam, 17, 19, 20, 21, 57

joint operations, 41

Korean War, 10, 11

lasers, 45, 54

missions, 5, 21, 41; antiterror, 52;
    assault, 12; bombing, 13, 21, 50;
    close air support, 45, 50, 52;
    combat, 33, 39, 40, 44; covert, 16,
    49; humanitarian, 44, 50, 52–53;
    infiltration and exfiltration, 10,
    11, 21, 36, 37, 49; search-and-
    rescue, 19, 21, 36, 40, 48

National Guard, 24, 44
Noriega, Manuel, 16–17, 56

officer training, 28–30, 40
Officer Training School, 28, 30

Panama, 16, 56
pararescue jumpers (PJs), 16, 25,
    34, 35, 41, 45, 53; missions, 5,
    13, 21, 48; motto, 48, 59;
    training, 11, 35, 38. *See also*
    special tactics squadrons
pararescuemen. *See* pararescue
    jumpers (PJs)
Persian Gulf War (1991), 17–19, 20,
    50, 57

al-Qaeda, 20, 57

radar, 17, 18, 36, 51
Reserve Officer Training Corps
     (ROTC), 28, 29

Scholastic Aptitude Test (SAT),
     28
SEALs. *See* U.S. Navy
smart helmets, 53
Somalia, 19
special operations, 4, 15
special tactics squadrons, 16, 34,
     40, 45. *See also* combat
     control technicians (CCTs);
     combat weathermen;
     pararescue jumpers (PJs)

terrorist attacks (September 11,
     2001), 19, 57
2003 Iraq war, 20, 57

unmanned aerial vehicle (UAV), 53
U.S. Air Force (USAF), 10, 11,
     12, 15, 17, 18, 22, 39, 56; 19;
     basic training, 31, 32–34; 1st
     Special Operations Wing
     (SOW), 16; 4400th Tactical
     Combat Crew Training
     Squadron, 12–13, 56;
     insignia, 46–47; require-
     ments, 24, 48; song, 31; 23rd
     Air Force, 16, 56; 2157th Air
     Rescue Service, 11; uniforms,
     26–27, 33
U.S. Air Force Special Operations
     Command (AFSOC): Aerospace
     Rescue and Recovery units,
     56; CCTs, 5, 12, 13, 14, 16, 20,
     21, 25, 34, 34, 41, 44, 45, 52;
     early history, 5–10, 56; 18th
     Flight Test Squadron, 51;
     emblem, 54; established, 17,
     56; headquarters, 40; jobs, 23,
     24–25, 30–31, 34, 40, 52; Life
     Support Shop, 52; motto, 54;
     919th Special Operations
Wing, 43; 193rd Special
     Operations Wing, 19, 30; in
     Persian Gulf War, 17–19; PJs,
     5, 11, 12, 13, 16, 19, 21, 25,
     34, 35, 38, 41, 48, 53;
     requirements, 22–23, 34, 38;
     16th Special Operations Wing,
     55; Special Operations School,
     40–41; Special Tactics Combat
     Weather Team, 39; structure,
     55; Tactic Group, 38; 352nd
     Special Operations Group, 55;
     353rd Special Operations
     group, 55; training, 34–35,
     38–39, 40, 41; 24th Special
     tactics Squadron, 19; in 2003
     Iraq war, 20, 57; women, 23,
     25, 39, 40. *See also* U.S.
     Special Operations Command
     (USSOCOM)
U.S. Army, 6, 7, 11, 13, 15, 17,
     18, 59; Air Forces, 8, 10, 56;
     Delta Force, 59; 50th Aero
     Squadron, 6, 56; 1st Air
     Commando Group, 9; 160th
     Special Operations Aviation
     Regiment (SOAR), 43;
     Rangers, 5, 8, 16, 41
U.S. Military Academy at West
     Point, 28
U.S. Naval Academy, 28
U.S. Navy, 7, 15, 17; SEALs, 41
U.S. Special Operations
     Command (USSOCOM), 17

Vietnam War, 12–14, 53, 56, 57

warfare: conventional, 4;
     psychological operations
     (PSYOP), 16, 19, 30, 50, 56
weapons, 33, 37, 45, 49, 50, 54;
     bombs, 53. *See also* aircraft;
     helicopters
World War I, 5, 56, 59
World War II, 6–10, 11, 56, 59

## ABOUT THE AUTHOR

Award-winning author Jeremy Roberts has written numerous books for children. His book *King Arthur* was an NCSS/CBC Notable Children's Trade Book in the Field of Social Studies and a Bank Street College Best Children's Book of the Year. Other works by Roberts span a wide range of subjects, including the Beatles, Saint Joan of Arc, George Washington, Abraham Lincoln, and Franklin Delano Roosevelt. Roberts has also written several installments of the *Eerie, Indiana* television series and some horror tales. Jeremy Roberts lives with his wife and son in upstate New York.

## PHOTO ACKNOWLEDGMENTS

The images in the book are used with the permission of: courtesy of the United States Air Force, pp. 4, 5, 11, 12, 18, 21, 22, 23, 25, 27 (top), 29 (both), 30, 32, 34, 36 (both), 37 (top), 38, 40, 42, 43, 44, 46 (all), 47 (all), 48 (both), 51, 52, 54; courtesy of the National Archives (W&C 127), p. 7; courtesy of the Library of Congress (LC-USE6-D-008299), p. 8; © Bettmann/CORBIS, p. 14; © Photri, Inc., p. 26 (top); Defense Visual Information Center, pp. 26 (bottom), 27 (bottom), 33; © Colt Defense LLC, 37 (bottom); © CORBIS, p. 45.

Cover: courtesy of the United States Air Force.